Taking Weight Problems to School

By Michelle L. Dean

JayJo Books, L.L.C.
Publishing Special Books for Special Kids®

Taking Weight Problems to School
© 2005 JayJo Books, LLC
Edited by Karen Schader, Michelle Yannes & Christine Molino

Published by
JayJo Books, LLC
A Brand of Sunburst Visual Media
Publishing Special Books for Special Kids®

JayJo Books is a publisher of books to help teachers, parents, and children cope with chronic illnesses, special needs, and health education in classroom, family, and social settings.

Library of Congress Control Number: 2004116324
ISBN 1-891383-29-9
First Edition
Eighteenth book in our *Special Kids in School*® series

For all information, including
Premium and Special Sales, contact:
JayJo Books
P.O. Box 9120
Plainview, NY 11803-9020
1-800-999-6884
jayjobooks@guidancechannel.com
www.jayjo.com

The opinions in this book are solely those of the author. Medical care is highly individualized and should never be altered without professional medical consultation.

About the Author

Michelle L. Dean, MA, ATR-BC, LPC is a board-certified art psychotherapist and a licensed professional counselor who specializes in the treatment of eating disorders, body image acceptance, and survivors of trauma in her private practice in Glenside, Pennsylvania. In addition to her practice, she is an Adjunct Professor at Arcadia University, teaching art therapy courses.

Ms. Dean has presented extensively on the therapeutic benefits of art therapy with eating-disordered clients and has provided numerous workshops and trainings on the therapeutic uses of art for mental health clinicians. It is her hope that this book will be used to begin the dialog between teachers, parents, and children about eating disorder prevention and to increase sensitivity to body image issues.

Hi! My name is Tina. Purple is my favorite color. I have purple pants, shirts and dresses. My hairbrush and toothbrush are purple, and I'm sure you can guess what color my hair ribbons are! I love to learn about different countries, paint pictures and roller-blade — I even have purple skates.

It's morning, and I am getting ready for school. Not too long ago, I didn't like getting dressed for school, because I didn't feel pretty when I looked in the mirror.

That's because I am overweight.

My best friend Emily told me I was a good artist and smart and a really great friend. I knew there were a lot of good things about me, but sometimes it was really hard for me to see them. Because I was overweight, I sometimes felt really different from other kids. The worse I felt about myself, the more I wanted to eat. The more I ate, the more weight I gained.

Then I felt even more unhappy.

I didn't eat too much at just one meal; I ate too much almost all the time. It was hard for me to keep up with the other kids in gym class. When I had to run, I'd get out of breath, and I always felt really clumsy. Sometimes, it was hard to find clothes that fit me.

When I felt sad, my mom or dad tried to make me feel better by giving me sweet things to eat, like cookies or cake. Chocolate cake was my favorite.

Now my parents and I are learning better ways to help me when I'm sad!

I belong to a group for kids who have problems with their weight. Eric is never picked for any of the sports teams. Hannah says that being overweight makes her lonely. Katie is average size, but she is very afraid of becoming fat. When Katie is upset, she eats lots and lots of food. That's called binging. Binging makes Katie feel so guilty that she throws up what she's eaten. Ms. Joanne, the therapist who meets with us, says that the way Katie feels and acts is called "bulimia" (bull-ee-me-a).

In our group, we find ways to talk about what bothers us. Talking about my feelings makes it easier for me to eat the right amount of food.

My friend Emily is also in Ms. Joanne's group. Emily isn't overweight but she thinks she is, and her parents are very worried about her. Emily's older sister Megan was in the hospital last year, because she had an eating problem called "anorexia." Even though she was very thin, Megan was afraid to eat because she did not want to gain weight. She ate so little that she felt weak and dizzy. She couldn't even do her schoolwork. At the hospital, Megan learned to start eating normally again.

Ms. Joanne told us that some kids try to make themselves feel better by eating too little or too much.

Do you know what a nutritionist (new-trish-un-ist) is? It's someone who teaches people about healthy eating. Ms. Heather is my nutritionist, and she made a special food plan just for me to make sure I get enough of all the different foods my body needs. To help me follow my plan, we always keep healthy foods at home.

Ms. Heather taught me a really great trick about portions, and I'll share it with you: One serving of meat should be no bigger than the palm of my hand.

On my food plan, I can even have some treats—like my favorite chocolate cake.

Ms. Heather says it is important for my family to eat together at least once a day. Eating together helps me follow my eating plan. We eat healthy foods and the right size portions. My mom and dad really help me make good choices about food.

We all decided to spend less time watching television and on the computer. Instead, we do fun things together, like riding our bikes or going for a long walk every day. Being with my family makes me feel great!

Now, when I feel sad, Mom offers me a hug instead of something sweet.

Sometimes, kids tease me about my weight. When they call me names, it really hurts my feelings.

It also makes me feel bad when kids watch what I eat. I've learned which food choices are good for me and which ones are not. I may not always be able to follow my food plan perfectly, but it's up to me to get back to it or to ask for help if I need it.

When I feel good about myself, it helps me follow my food plan.

Ms. Jamie, my school nurse, says that kids come in all colors, shapes and sizes. She says it is a good thing that we are all different, but there are things that everyone needs in order to be healthy — a variety of foods in the right amount, plenty of water to drink, exercise and lots of love and respect.

And guess what? Even if we all eat and exercise the same amount, we are still going to be different sizes.

Here's how you can help me or other kids who have weight problems. I like to have friends, so please be my friend. Try to think about ways we are alike. Talk to me about what I do well or what you like about me, not about what I look like.

And if you love the color purple like I do, tell me. I'll even share my favorite purple marker with you!

Now, when I look in the mirror, I can smile at myself. I know that I am trying hard to be healthy by eating well, drinking lots of water and exercising. Gym class has gotten easier, too. And I always remember what Ms. Jamie says…

Kids come in all colors, sizes and shapes and that's okay!

TAKE THE KIDS' QUIZ!

1. **How did being overweight make Tina feel?**
   Tina felt different from the other kids. It was hard for her to see the good things about herself.

2. **What is binging?**
   Binging is eating a very large amount of food.

3. **What is anorexia?**
   Some kids think they are overweight even if they aren't. Because they are afraid to gain weight, they eat so little food that they may feel weak and dizzy. Kids with anorexia need professional help to learn how to eat normally.

4. **What does a nutritionist do?**
   A nutritionist is someone who teaches people about healthy eating.

5. **How does having a food plan help Tina?**
   Tina's food plan makes sure that she gets enough of all of the different foods her body needs, and in the right amounts.

6. **Is it okay if Tina has chocolate cake or other treats?**

Tina can have some treats and still follow her food plan. She's learned which food choices are good and which aren't, and if she doesn't follow her food plan perfectly, it's up to her to get back to it.

7. **How does Tina's family help her manage her weight?**

Tina's mom and dad help her make good choices about what she eats by keeping healthy food in their house, and they set a good example for her by eating properly. The family exercises together, too.

8. **How can you help kids with weight problems?**

If you know kids who have weight problems, be a friend. Think about ways you are alike. Talk about what they do well or what you like about them, not about what they look like.

9. **What are some things we all need to be healthy?**

Everyone needs a variety of foods in the right amount, plenty of water to drink, exercise and lots of love and respect.

10. **Is it okay for kids to be different?**

Yes! We all come in different colors, sizes and shapes and that's okay!

TEN TIPS FOR TEACHERS

✓ **1. Promote Healthy Eating and Exercise Habits.**
Helping students form healthy eating and exercise habits can go a long way to preventing weight problems in their lives. Eating behaviors and nutrition affect not only their physical well-being, but also their emotional well-being.

✓ **2. Provide Empowerment.**
Promote a climate of empowerment through acceptance of individuality and differences. Challenge media and advertising messages that advocate a single body type as healthy or desirable and promote body dissatisfaction to sell products or services. A classroom where students feel they can address issues of self-esteem, body image and pressures openly is valuable. Seek more support through speakers and curriculum, if needed.

✓ **3. Distinguish the Person from the Body.**
Promote an environment that values children for all their unique personal qualities and not for their appearance alone. Children who are struggling with a weight problem will benefit from feeling accepted and supported.

✓ **4. Be a Role Model for Your Students.**
Model acceptance and respect for your own body and those of others. Be particularly careful about conveying unintentional messages, such as expressing dissatisfaction with your own body or making disparaging remarks about other people's bodies. These messages have an effect on your students.

✓ **5. Recognize the Signs of Eating Disorders.**
A child with a weight issue may experiment with restricting food, binging, and/or purging. Be alert to these patterns of behavior; they may be symptoms of a developing, or full-blown, eating disorder. Become familiar with the symptoms of anorexia nervosa and bulimia nervosa and with patterns of compulsive overeating.

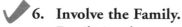

6. Involve the Family.

Family involvement is crucial in promoting understanding and changing lifestyle patterns in children and teenagers. Eating disorders affect everyone in a family, and family members can be the most positive influence for young people. Educate families about resources in the community that specialize in the treatment of children with eating disorders and weight issues.

7. Start a Support Group.

Provide a safe place for students to explore peer pressure and media pressure in our weight-conscious society. Eating disorders have been found to develop at younger ages than drug and alcohol use and are more lethal. Given the opportunity and support, students can create their own climate of acceptance.

8. Encourage Parents to Seek Professional Help For Their Children.

Like many illnesses, the sooner eating-disordered behaviors are treated the better the prognosis. This is especially true for children. Become familiar with the professionals in your area who are skilled and experienced in treating children with eating disorders and weight issues, and suggest that parents enlist their assistance quickly.

9. Deter Teasing.

Children with weight problems are likely to suffer from poor self-image and low self-esteem, and teasing and name-calling can be extremely destructive to them. Do not tolerate teasing, as it creates an unsafe climate for all students.

10. Recognize That Dieting is Not the Answer.

Dieting, as well as compulsive exercise and other radical attempts to control body weight, are not the solution to children's weight problems. The practices and the attitudes that support them are harmful and can create even more problems. Discourage behaviors and attitudes that place a premium on appearance, perfection or performance beyond what is reasonable for the age group. Provide a focus on healthy patterns of eating and exercise combined with other activities that enhance self-acceptance and self-esteem.

ADDITIONAL RESOURCES

National Eating Disorders Association (NEDA)
603 Stewart Street, Suite 803
Seattle, WA 98101-1264
800.931.2237
206.382.3587
www.nationaleatingdisorders.org

National Association of Anorexia Nervosa and Associated Disorders (ANAD)
P.O. Box 7
Highland Park, IL 60035
847.831.3438
www.anad.org

Anorexia Nervosa and Related Eating Disorders, Inc. (ANRED)
P.O. Box 5102
Eugene, OR 97405
541.344.1144
www.anred.com

American Academy of Pediatrics
141 Northwest Point Boulevard
Elk Grove Village, IL 60007
847.434.4000
www.aap.org

National Center for Chronic Disease Prevention and Health Promotion
Division of Nutrition and Physical Activity
4770 Buford Highway, NE, MS/K-2
Atlanta, GA 30341
770.488.5820
www.cdc.gov/nccdphp/dnpa

To order additional copies of this book or inquire about our quantity discounts for schools, hospitals, and affiliated organizations, contact us at 1-800-999-6884.

From our *Special Kids in School*® series
Taking A.D.D. to School
Taking Arthritis to School
Taking Asthma to School
Taking Autism to School
Taking Cancer to School
Taking Cerebral Palsy to School
Taking Cystic Fibrosis to School
Taking Depression to School
Taking Diabetes to School
Taking Down Syndrome to School
Taking Dyslexia to School
Taking Food Allergies to School
Taking Hearing Impairment to School
Taking Seizure Disorders to School
Taking Speech Disorders to School
Taking Tourette Syndrome to School
Taking Visual Impairment to School
Taking Weight Problems to School
...and others coming soon!

From our *Healthy Habits for Kids*® series
There's a Louse in My House
A Fun Story about Kids and Head Lice

From our *Special Family and Friends*™ series
Allie Learns About Alzheimer's Disease
A Family Story about Love, Patience, and Acceptance
Patrick Learns About Parkinson's Disease
A Story of a Special Bond Between Friends
Dylan Learns About Diabetes

And from our *Substance Free Kids*® series
Smoking STINKS!!™
A Heartwarming Story about the Importance of Avoiding Tobacco

Other books available now!
SPORTSercise!
A School Story about Exercise-Induced Asthma
ZooAllergy
A Fun Story about Allergy and Asthma Triggers
Rufus Comes Home
Rufus the Bear with Diabetes™
A Story about Diagnosis and Acceptance
The ABC's of Asthma
An Asthma Alphabet Book for Kids of All Ages
Trick-or-Treat for Diabetes
A Halloween Story for Kids Living with Diabetes

A portion of the proceeds from all our publications is donated to various charities to help fund important medical research and education. We work hard to make a difference in the lives of children with chronic conditions and/or special needs. Thank you for your support.